Copyright ©2025 GOD IS WRITING MY STORY, NOT THE WORLD. Grace in Every Trial. A Memoir by Sylvia D. Mitchell. All rights reserved. No part of this book may be reproduced in any form or by any means, electronic, mechanical, photocopying, recording, or otherwise, without written permission of the publisher, except where permitted by law.

Cover Photo:
Sylvia D. Mitchell Archives

Beta Reader:
Christine Atherley

Cover Design / Book Layout:
Darlene Gist Graphic Design
www. dggd.biz
dggd@aol.com • shesmypublisher@aol.com

PRINTED IN U.S.A.
MMXXV

ISBN #:
979-8-218-89436-8

GOD IS WRITING MY STORY NOT THE WORLD
Grace in Every Trial

A Memoir By
Sylvia Diane Mitchell

To My Heavenly Father

This book is dedicated to You, who wrote my story before I lived it. I think of **Psalm 139:16,** reflecting on my life.

"All the days ordained for me were written in Your book before one of them came to be."

Every prayer, triumph, moment, had been planned by You, Father God, long before I knew it.

In every battle, trial or storm, You have already written the ending of my story.

And I gratefully thank You, my Lord and Savior, for the joyful ending of my life's story.

Amen.

Disclaimer

This memoir is based on true events, as I remember them.

While the truth of these experiences remains, certain names, relationships, and details have been changed to honor the privacy of others.

Any resemblance to actual persons living or deceased, is coincidental and unintentional.

Preface

What follows is a personal account of my spiritual journey, a testimony to the ways God has led, taught and transformed me.

At the heart, this Memoir is about learning that God is the author of my life, even when events seem chaotic or painful.

> *"For I know the plans I have for you. Plans to prosper you and not to harm you, plans to give you hope and a future."*
> **Jeremiah 29:11**

This scripture tells me that He has plans of a joyful ending for me.

My story has already been written by God, and every chapter leads to His hope for me.

Relying on God has brought me peace, when attempting to be self-reliant has caused me misery and anguish.

For years, I secretly suppressed the parts of my story that were too painful. I own my story now!

My mind is now renewed and my thoughts realigned, as God continues to shape me from the inside out.

I trust the story God has written for my life.

Prologue

"Ms. Mitchell, are you home yet?" Dr. Fine inquired through a voice seized with urgency.

I looked at my phone, as if scanning his face for clarification.

"No, I'm walking to my car," as I pivoted towards the direction of his office.

~~

I thought I knew what faith was.

As I revisit the chapters of my life that molded my thinking, I'm filled with gratitude to God for bringing me through and showing me a better way.

This event is a catalyst that shaped my perspective and influenced future chapters in my life.

Table of Contents

To My Heavenly Father i
Disclaimer iii
Preface v
Prologue vii
Forsaken 1
Oh, Law-dy 7
Drama and Trauma 11
For the Good 17
God Makes a Way 19
Searching and Seeking 23
Lost Sheep 29
It's a Part of Life 35
A Friend in Need 37
Faith Is Powerful 41
Lean on Him 47
Girls' Trip 53
The Turning Point 57
The Awakening 61
Thank You 65

CHAPTER ONE

Forsaken

"God is love; and he that dwelleth in love dwelleth in God, and God in him."
1 John 4:16 (NIV)

From a very young age, I believed no one cared enough to look after me. That belief hardened me early. I learned to depend only on myself, to keep my guard up, and to pretend I didn't need love even when my heart was starving for it.

The hurt was so deep and profound, and yet no one seemed to notice. I certainly didn't have the maturity or wisdom to recognize what I was really missing.

What others mistook for maturity and strength in me as a little girl, was a mask I used to survive. This mask was a defense mechanism activated and/or deactivated, depending upon the level of trauma experienced.

~~

When I was just five, my uncle became my guardian through the court system. The courts determined that my mother was incapable of raising her many kids.

I was told that my mom's mother passed away when she was young. Also, my dad and his mother had a disagreement about my father's life choices. Therefore, my visits to that grandmother were so few that I barely remember them. As circumstances unfolded, my uncle assumed guardianship of my sisters and me. That transition marked a significant turning point in our lives, one that reshaped our sense of family and stability.

I didn't realize then that God was seeing beyond my façade. He was watching over me, even when I felt I was all alone.

I came to live with my aunt as a 'package deal.' She wanted my uncle so desperately that she added me and my two older sisters to her four kids. I wouldn't call it a blended family, since I felt as if I never blended in.

Missing are memories of my life before I was taken away to live with my uncle and aunt.

There are no memories of being with my mother; her holding me or kissing me, no playing in a park, no favorite doll or anything of that sort.

It saddens me that my childhood memories are shaped more by whispers and rumors than by warmth, guidance, or certainty.

The only vague memory I have is of an old lady giving me fig newton cookies. All pre-five-year-old memories are blocked out as if inconsequential.

My aunt was jealous of the fact that my uncle had a friendly relationship with my mother. She outwardly disparaged my mother in my presence. She even had a nasty nickname for her, "Little F'k."

Taking a cue from their mother badmouthing my mom, her kids added salt to my wounds.

"Go home to your real mother," was the taunt when one of them were angry, jealous or just being a mean brat.

I vaguely recall my uncle taking me to visit my mother, but telling me to keep it our secret.

I remember one occasion when my uncle saw my aunt's kids doing their homework together on the living room floor.

"Have the kids help her with her homework," my uncle said.

He made an effort to fulfill the responsibility of a guardian. But when I discovered his deception toward both my mom and my aunt, he positioned me in a space that required God's protection and wisdom.

"She don't need help with homework. Her reading and writing is better than mine. That girl gets A's on all her tests. She can help my kids, she's smart, " my aunt said.

Though my two older sisters were with me, they had teenage lives of their own and were oblivious to my needs.

They were also in a new environment attempting to make new friends, and of course, meet new boys. Besides, it wasn't their obligation to take care of me.

My sisters had no idea that I was lost, lonely and hopelessly missed my mother. I also yearned for a grandmother that could hold and comfort me during these desolate times.

On school papers and applications, I was told by my aunt, to write her name in the space for 'mother.' This essentially was an attempt to erase my mother from my life. I was perplexed and confused, wondering if my mom was still my mother.

Without therapy or counseling, I carried experiences no child should have had to navigate alone. I felt as if I was ripped from my mother's arms and placed in the care of apathetic, detached and emotionally deficient caregivers.

Growing up motherless, I yearned for love, affection and tenderness. Sadly, my needs were never met.

I felt alone, abandoned, and tossed aside like a worn out, bald, one-eyed rag doll.

~~

As a teenager, I always worked – either as a babysitter or for a neighborhood youth program. I stashed my money until my aunt found out, and asked to borrow it. The loans were never repaid.

One day, I asked for a new pair of deck sneakers.

"You don't need me to buy your clothes, you got money," she said.

From the age of fourteen, I bought my own clothes.

During a 'secret visit' to my mother, I asked my mom to buy me something. "You're not on my budget," she replied.

Who could I turn to when I needed something, if not the adults in my life? I had no anchor, no solid ground. But God never took his eyes off of me.

CHAPTER TWO

Oh, Law-dy

"And we know that for those who love God all things work together for good..."
Romans 8:28 (NIV)

I always loved school. My vocational high school prepared me well for the job market. Courses in typing, stenography, bookkeeping and advanced English, landed me a 'good job' in a prestigious law firm after graduation.

Being proficient in Pitman shorthand, I got a position working for a Managing Partner of a law firm.

Working with Mr. Manco was financially rewarding and strengthened my self-confidence. But not everyone appreciated my role in the firm.

One day, I returned from lunch fifteen minutes late. The receptionist came to me with the sign-in sheet in hand.

"Look, Mr. Levy circled the time you signed in from lunch and showed it to Mr. Manco. Girl, for some reason, he has it in for you. Be careful," she whispered.

She hid the sheet in a magazine and trotted back to the reception desk.

Mr. Levy was a new Associate in the firm, fresh out of law school. His father was well-respected in a Brooklyn synagogue. It was rumored that Mr. Levy didn't like the fact that someone with my melanin-rich skin could obtain this position.

"Can you come in a for minute," Mr. Manco asked upon my return from lunch one day.

Oh, shit.

"Yes," I closed his door.

"Levy is complaining about how much time you spend at lunch, and also that you're on the phone a lot."

"Tom, I sometimes am a little late back from lunch, but…"

"Sylvia, don't worry about it. He seems to disapprove of us working together. I told him that you do your work efficiently and I have no problem with you. Just ease up on the phone a little, okay?"

I relayed the conversation in the breakroom to Cindy, a co-worker.

"Listen, you know the scripture Isaiah 54:17?" she asked.

"No, I really don't know any except the 23rd Psalm," I confessed.

"Well, look it up and say it before you come to work and at your desk also. Watch what happens."

I took her advice and began to repeat, "No weapon formed against me shall prosper," several times during my work hours.

~~

"Hi, Sylvia. It's Cindy," she excitedly announced herself.

"Cindy, you're calling me on my vacation? What's up?"

I picked up the remote and paused the movie I was watching.

"Didn't I tell you God don't like ugly and he will turn things around."

"I don't get it, Cindy. What in the world are you talking about?"

"I'm talking about the prejudice-ass, just got out of law school, jealous Associate Levy. His ass got fired," Cindy squealed.

"Stop it. What?"

"He missed the filing date of some court papers and the partners booted him," she said.

"You serious? I guess prayer does work."

"Of course it does. You gotta have faith, girl," she said.

I continued to work for Tom for ten years, after which he branched out and established his own law firm. I subsequently joined him as Office Manager, and received a huge salary increase.

I have learned that God turns every scheme against me into a blessing to prove His faithfulness. What others plan for my harm, He beautifully and gently reshapes for my good and His glory.

Now, it's my turn to let Him reshape how I think and live, and trust Him in every aspect of my life.

CHAPTER THREE

Drama and Trauma

"Finally, all of you, be like-minded, be sympathetic, love one another, be compassionate and humble."
1 Peter 3:8 (NIV)

Meanwhile, my relationship with my live-in boyfriend, Bobby is toxic and dysfunctional.

In addition, we are financially deficient, a foregone conclusion when one half of a partnership doesn't pull their weight.

One Thursday, I receive a phone call at work from a neighbor.

"Ms. Mitchell, this is Daniel in 23C. Everything is fine now but your son is laying in the street. He was hit by a car."

As I sprint past Tom's desk, holding back tears, I yell, "I'm leaving. My son was hit by a car."

I meet the ambulance at the hospital, and observe the car tire tracks on my crying son's right leg. It was devastating. My son had been chasing his friend into the street between parked cars. The driver didn't see him.

And where is his father? Upstairs asleep while my 8-year-old son is outside, unsupervised.

Another day, while I'm a work, and of course, Bobby is home. He, again, got fired because the boss 'had it in for him.'

"Ms. Mitchell, we're sorry but we had to take your son to the police station. Once again, he had not been picked up from school, and the teachers waited as long as they could. You can pick him up at the 71st Precinct."

And where is his father? Home asleep.

Bobby never kept a job long enough for the ink to dry on a job application.

I paid the rent and bills; lying awake at night trying to figure out how to survive. I hear him snoring peacefully, while I'm in agony.

I knew something had to change when one evening, I stood over a sleeping Bobby and plotted how to kill him. I knew where he kept the stash of guns, and he slept very soundly. I just had to shoot him in his sleep. It was a scary proposition, but I was being pushed over the edge.

I had endured many circumstances that told me to get away from Bobby.

I'm so grateful that I finally paid attention to God's nudge to change my situation, but not in a way that would hurt anyone. God never intended me to live beneath my worth.

He designed me for joy, peace and abundance. I was ready to claim what He had always meant for me to have.

I had continually allowed Bobby to steal my Peace and Joy. Deceptively, he is very handsome, well-educated and cordial to our neighbors. Too cordial, as I discovered that he was fooling around with several of them.

A handsome exterior is no substitute for moral character, of which Bobby woefully lacked.

On one occasion, a neighbor said:

"Your boyfriend is so fine. He reminds me of Richard Roundtree in the movie Shaft."

I thought to myself, "Yep, there's another one."

Fear, threats of physical harm, and embarrassment held me hostage in this unhealthy relationship. The thought of me harming someone terrified me. I needed a solution that would not jeopardize the lives of me and my sons. I prayed, "Lord, please help me."

~~

That year, Bobby had an upcoming Family Reunion. Of course, the man in my household did not have money for an airline ticket.

We argued, as usual. Bobby wanted me to pay the rent late and buy him a ticket. This would mean that I would now be two months behind in the rent.

I decided to buy tickets for me and my boys, and didn't give in to his demands. My money, my solution.

While I attended his reunion and he didn't, Bobby incessantly phoned and cursed me out. His mother encouraged me to ignore him.

"He's wrong as two left shoes. I don't care if he is my son, you need to get rid of his sorry ass."

Those words of encouragement from his mother reached me at a time when I needed them most. They gave me the strength and freedom to finally move on.

The boys and I had a great time. The accommodations, amusement park and food were magnificent.

"Are we rich?" my younger son asked one morning, while in the pool.

"No, but I work hard so you can enjoy good things in life. If you want to have or be something in life, you have to take steps to achieve it."

I had my first son at age 20, and the second at 27 years old. I poured my life and all the love I knew into my sons, giving them what my heart longed for at their age. Where there were gaps in my own upbringing, I chose to plant love.

I thank God for them every day, recognizing them as gifts entrusted to me. I pray they continue to live, walk, and grow in love rooted in Him.

I trusted that God would guide my words to reach my sons' ears. I wanted to protect them from adopting their father's lack of ambition and drive.

We delighted in the crab boils filled with corn, potatoes, sausages, and whatever else his family piled into the industrial-sized stock pots. It really felt like family, with everybody sitting on a floor covered with newspaper and crab shells.

The boys and I enjoyed a fun time in Miami, while my boyfriend sought pleasure in other activities.

~~

Returning home from the reunion, I didn't see Bobby for a week. He didn't even call. When he came home, I confronted him about his absence.

"What you gonna do about it. Kick my ass?" he said.

I had no internal weaponry; no strength or confidence to combat this mental and physical mistreatment. I felt fear, anxiety and a foreboding angst.

I couldn't sleep that night. I lay in bed with my face to the wall and prayed. Even as I prayed, I was afraid that darkness was about to descend.

Lord, I place every worry in Your hands. You are in control.

When Bobby left in the morning to play his illegal 'numbers,' I called a friend to rescue me. I threw some clothes in a bag and picked the boys up from school.

This time, I wasn't home when Bobby returned. I went into hiding for two weeks.

I had a plan in mind when I decided to come back home. What I thought would be a return to normal, turned out to be a new beginning shaped by His loving hands.

CHAPTER FOUR

For the Good

"Forget the former things; do not dwell on the past. See, I am doing a new thing! Now it springs up; do you not perceive it?"
Isaiah 43:18 (NIV)

For my security, a few family members met me at the house when I returned. Though Bobby could be unpredictable, he was on his best behavior, pulling out his stash of marijuana and chatting them up.

We were sitting around the table: my two brothers, a sister, my nephew and two friends. Bobby believed it was just another get together.

Bobby had an abundance of marijuana separated from the seeds, on an album cover. My two 'enforcers', a nephew and a brother, helped to roll the joints.

Bobby thinks the party is on!

My sister, Betty, suddenly stood up, hovering over my brother Craig, who was blowing a ring of smoke from his joint.

In a flash, with a deliberate fling of the wrist, Betty tosses some papers across the table at Bobby.

He looked at the legal documents, flabbergasted and annoyed.

"What the hell is this?"

"You have been served," Betty flashed a smirk, enjoying every minute of her delivery.

"Really. This is what we do?" Bobby said, glaring at me.

He then threw the "Notice to Vacate Premises" across the table, missing my face.

"Yo man, you know what time it is," Craig said, standing up.

Bobby then grabbed a few joints off the table and bolted to the bedroom; never to be seen for the rest of the evening.

~~

A few days later, Bobby packed up most of his belongings and relocated. I assume he moved in with one of the multiple women he was "entangled" with.

I subsequently discovered that he confiscated most of our family photos, and of course, the guns he had stashed in the apartment.

What Bobby didn't know was that the Lord had given me wisdom, courage and a plan to break from his abuse.

Fear was once my master, but God became my Savior. He lifted me out of that valley, but the journey was far from over.

CHAPTER FIVE

God Makes a Way

For the Lord your God is He who goes with you to fight for you against your enemies, to give you the victory.
Deuteronomy 20:4 (NIV)

What a relief! A weight is lifted. I'm enjoying coming home after work. No questions, no fights or arguments if I'm five minutes late, according to Bobby's calculation.

No more watching him jump up from his 'office chair,' the couch, when I came through the door ladened with groceries for dinner.

Bobby was gone, and so was the trepidation that ruled over me for years.

So, I thought!

Leaving for work one day, I'm locking the door and walking toward the elevator.

Bobby jumps from behind the staircase and grabs me by the arm.

"Bitch, I don't care about no damn vacate papers. I will kick your ass here, and see what those punk ass cops do then."

He proceeds to taunt and verbally abuse me the three blocks to the train station, and onto the train where he continues to whisper threats in my ear.

When my stop came, I sprinted to the door and rushed through the crowd.

"You think it's that easy. You just wait," he yelled as the door closed.

~~

For months, Bobby pleaded to come back home. Between the abusive tirades, apologies, crying and pornographic phone calls, it took several years until Bobby, sort of, accepted the fact that I was no longer 'his'.

Subsequently, he replaced me with another mistress – drugs. The substances kept him occupied for quite some time. Bobby was so consumed with feeding his habit, that he didn't have time or energy to work. Obviously, I couldn't collect child support from a salary that he never received.

The sad truth is that I'm not accustomed to Bobby financially or emotionally supporting me anyway.

My days were spent in the daily grind: work, home, homework, cooking, bed, get up and repeat. Once again, I feel afraid, lost and lonely.

I didn't truly have a relationship with God back then, but I could sense His presence moving quietly through my life. Those were the nudges I was feeling. He was opening paths, closing doors and protecting me from things I couldn't see. I didn't know Him, but He knew me. He always did.

CHAPTER SIX

Searching and Seeking

"The Lord is near the brokenhearted and saves the crushed in spirit."
Psalm 34:18 (NIV)

One day at a business training, I was speaking with a church member.

"Wasn't service good?" I said.

"Yes, Pastor really broke down the meaning of being a Christian. You going next week?"

"Yeah, see you then," I said turning to walk away.

Out of I don't know where, came Joe. He was fairly new to the business.

"I want to go to church with you," he said, approaching us.

That's how my relationship with Joe began. With our first date being at church.

He was recently divorced and restarting his life. We became a couple quickly, and were recognized as partners in the business.

Joe would work during the day, stay at my house overnight, and leave early in the morning before my sons woke up.

One morning, Joe got out of the bed to make a phone call. I have always been a very light sleeper, and therefore, heard the conversation.

"Sheryl, you up? You up?" he whispered.

I had a feeling that something was going on with them. Call it "woman's intuition."

"What was that about?" I said when he returned to the bedroom.

"Oh, she just asked me to wake her up for the morning meeting."

"Why does she need you to wake her up?"

"We're just being supportive teammates. I would do that for anybody," was his excuse.

"Do I have anything to worry about?" I asked, not expecting the truth.

"No babe, I'm just helping a teammate because she's always late."

There were hints along the way, like breadcrumbs leading to the truth. I already knew, but refused to accept the truth. I didn't want to lose him.

I went away on a trip and called him to say hello. He told me that I should enjoy myself and shouldn't be calling him. Strange.

Another time was on New Year's Eve. I naturally expected to hang out with my man. When I called him to get ready, he told me that he wanted to stay home. Really? Another hint that he had other plans with another person.

~~

One evening while sitting in the kitchen, I posed a question that I had been afraid to ask him.

"Babe, where do you see this going? My boys aren't stupid. They're going to realize that you stay here sometimes."

Without skipping a beat, as if he had contemplated this scenario, he answered me.

"Well, I can't see that far down the road," he said.

That evening in bed, I told Joe that I wasn't going to shack up in front of my sons. It took me years to have a boyfriend in their presence. I wanted my sons to respect me. I suggested that we take a break to figure us out.

Again, Joe appeared to have contemplated this scenario also.

"I'll leave in the morning," he said, turning his back to me.

Tears began pouring from me onto the pillow. I was shocked by the immediacy of his answer.

"I don't mean to break up permanently. I just mean that we should take a minute to work on a plan," I cried, I pleaded, I begged!

When he packed up his things to leave, I noticed that he went to a room with a closet that I never used. The door would get stuck and hard to open.

Joe opened the door, with ease, and removed about ten white work shirts and five pair of pants. I have heard about men sneakily moving in with women without their knowledge. I thought, how clueless are these women not to see that. Now, look at me!

Unbeknownst to me, Joe had actually moved his clothes in, right under my nose, and I had no idea!

Reflecting back, I had lost sight of who I was. With no sense of self-worth, I settled for attention that wasn't love, just so I wouldn't feel alone.

Looking back on that season of my life, I can see how God was quietly revealing my true worth. Even when Bobby couldn't recognize the value in me, God was steadily reminding me that I was more than the way I was being treated.

What Bobby failed to affirm, God affirmed with a confidence and love that began to reshape how I saw myself.

~~

Some time later, actually two weeks, our business team was on a plane headed for New Orleans, Louisiana.

The atmosphere was electric with excitement. The team visited New Orleans before, and envisioned the exhilaration of Bourbon Street, Gumbo and the alcohol-potent, Hurricane drink.

After several requests to clear the aisles, we sat down in our seats.

Suddenly, I notice Joe, which is no surprise since he's a team member. He was putting his carry-on bag in the overhead compartment, and then sat down next to another teammate.

Then came a heart-wrenching episode that shook my foundation.

Joe and Sheryl landed in seats two rows in front of me. Joe whispered to her. Simultaneously, they turn around to look at me. *And he said I had nothing to worry about.*

Sheryl then rubs the back of his head and smiles at me. It was the most cunning, wicked smile I have ever encountered.

The river of tears I cried were too profound to internalize. My uncontrollable wailing exposed an agonizing, inconsolable pain.

The couple buckled their seatbelts and settled into their flight, care-free. Joe and Sheryl thought nothing of shattering my heart into a million fragments. Shards of my broken heart spilled into the aisle, to be trampled on repeatedly.

My cries of anguish were so loud, a flight attendant came forward. She led me to her jump seat at the back of the plane. Compassionately, she rested my head on her shoulder, and allowed me to pour my tears onto her uniform.

I plotted revenge, believing it would ease the hurt I carried. I wanted them to feel the pain they caused me. But God was quietly mending the broken pieces of my soul instead.

"I have a lot of dirt on him. I can get him in real trouble."

"Girl, don't even think about that. God says 'It is mine to avenge. I will repay.'

"Leave that dog to his bone. He'll get his," the flight attendant said.

~~

"Who is this? I asked the gasping, sobbing voice on the phone.

He sniffled between words. "It's me, can you talk?"

What's up?" I said with an unforgiving attitude.

"If I hurt you as much as I am hurting now, I apologize. I am so sorry," he bawled.

Joe tells me his tale of woes. He moved in with Sheryl, which confirmed to me that he was shacking from woman to woman. He was a philanderer who charmed women, and then moved in with them rent-free.

Joe and Sheryl's working schedules were like ships passing in the night. But that day, he comes home early to find Sheryl and another teammate in their bed!

Some may say "what goes around, comes around."

I lean more towards "you reap what you sow." I believe that if you do good, you'll receive good.

I pray that Joe learned from his pain and transformed his exploitative behavior.

I am learning that what God wants for me, He will make happen in His time and in His way.

I no longer indulge in behaviors or promiscuities that diminish my self-worth. Nor do I chase after people or things that don't encourage or inspire me. The Lord showed me that I am more than what I once accepted, and I deserve better than what I settled for.

God truly is in control, and His plans are always better than mine.

CHAPTER SEVEN

Lost Sheep

"If I had one sheep out of all of them that was missing, I would do everything I could to find, to rescue, that one sheep."
Luke 15:3-7 (NIV)

"**P**eter keeps calling like a relentless bee. Or like that gnat that you can't kill. I just can't get rid of him," I complained to Madeline, my best friend of over 40 years.

Our long-time friend was persistent in requesting me to accompany him to church. He 'found the Lord' after many years of living an alcohol and drug-induced existence. Now he thinks everybody should find what he discovered. I wasn't feeling it. And especially all this 'church stuff.'

"Come go to church with me. I'll pick you up at 9:00," the voicemail said.

I picked up the phone and agreed to go with him. If not, he would just keep calling - like a Witness.

I went to church with Peter three weeks in a row and decided it was enough.

Like clockwork, he called at 7pm on a Saturday night to put in his request.

"I went with you last week. You don't even have any eligible men to introduce me to," I said.

"Girl, you go to church for salvation, not "pal-vation."

"Ok, but I am not going next week," I threatened.

I realize the Lord sent Peter to help me build a relationship with Him, but I just wasn't ready.

When I reflect on my childhood, I never saw any adult in my life walk into a church.

The only time I ever went to church, was with my Hispanic friends when I was 8 years old. They went to a Catholic church, and I tagged along as a social event.

I even received my Communion and Confirmation as a course of the friendship. But we were not a family of church-goers.

When I got home from church, I called Madeline.

"Listen, I live in Brooklyn. You live in the Bronx near Peter and he's your good friend also. You should share in the job of going to church with him, too."

"Job?" Madeline giggled.

"That's what I feel like. I have to put the time in every week. I'm sick of this fanatic calling me Saturday evenings to go to church with him on Sundays. I'm afraid to answer my phone."

"He said when people call him a fanatic, he tells them that it means he's a fan of God," Madeline said.

"Well, I'm sick of Mr. Fanatic calling me when I'm nursing a hangover. I'm not going to stop saving seats for my squad at the bar. That's our spot. And if I can't find a friend in church, maybe there's one waiting for me at the bar. Damn, he's worse than an ex-smoker that suddenly can't stand the smell of smoke. I'm gonna change my number!" I said.

Two weeks after imploring her, Madeline did me the favor and attended church with Peter. In time, she caught the 'church bug' which had a positive influence on my attitude regarding our 'fanatic' friend.

Eventually, Peter and Madeline's friendship evolved into a courtship and a few years later, a marriage. I gave my blessing to my two life-long friends, knowing that what God ordains, He also sustains.

~~

One Sunday, the Pastor did an alter call for people who wanted prayer for deliverance from addictions, unforgiveness, loneliness, abusive behaviors, etc.

That day, the three of us went to church together. Madeline was sitting next to me, while Peter was singing with the choir.

After the choir sang, "Friend of God," the Pastor said:

"If you don't have a relationship with Jesus, and want that, please come forward. If you would like to accept Jesus Christ as your Lord and Savior, come up to the alter. Take that walk of faith and come now."

The choir sang, and I hear a whisper for me to surrender.

Suddenly, I felt the Holy Spirit's nudge, guiding me to move forward in faith.

I then grabbed Madeline's hand and floated up to the alter.

On November 18, 1990, I accepted Jesus as my Lord and Savior. I began reading the Bible for the first time in my life. As a 'newbie' in the Word, I began with the Gospel of John.

Since then, I have accomplished reading the entire Bible in a year, to challenge my commitment to learning the Word of God.

I recall being new in my Spiritual Walk, when Madeline asked me what I was sacrificing for Lent.

"I ain't doing that. I'm not ready to give up things I enjoy. God knows my heart," I said.

Thankfully, I'm not the same person – I think and feel differently now because of God.

For years after guiding me to salvation, the 'pain in the neck' Peter, served as a 'fisher of men'. He was like a fisherman, who instead, caught men as his mission. His purpose was to lead men to a relationship with God and His teachings.

He has since transitioned to be with the Lord.

As in Matthew 25:23, a Master replied:

"Well done, my good and faithful servant."

I am sure the Lord is pleased with Peter's ministry. I'm forever grateful to him. I resisted every step, yet God was waiting at the end of the road.

During my journey, I learned that faith in God doesn't shield you from trials and tribulations. But faith does give you strength to endure them.

The impending storm would be more than a trial. It was the biggest test of my faith, the one that taught me what true trust in God really meant.

CHAPTER EIGHT

It's a Part of Life

"For if we live, we live to the Lord, and if we die, we die to the Lord. So then, whether we live or whether we die, we are the Lord's."
Romans 14:8 (KJV)

It's really a blur. People attempt to force some memories out of me, but I can't recall.

"Remember when the lady fell on the casket?"

"No, I don't," I say.

"Remember when the drunk guy was talking too much? You have to remember that."

"I do not remember," I snapped.

I had four family deaths within three months. From March 2007 through May 2007, the worse time in my life.

In that short period of time, I lost my parents and two sisters.

Before my heart, my mind and soul could regroup, I was planning funerals of my two brothers who passed two weeks apart.

Six obituaries later, the trauma left me broken and weary. I was battling depression and emotional pain I could hardly bear.

But even in the darkest places, God never abandoned me.

I knew God could handle my pain, as always. Still, my heart was hurting.

Upon reflection, I realized that God, in His mercy, hid certain memories from me. It was not to keep me in denial, but to protect me while He prepared me for healing.

CHAPTER NINE

A Friend in Need

"For he shall give his angels charge over thee to keep thee in all thy ways..."
Psalm 91:11 (KJV)

Months after the deaths, I was driving to my friend, Clara's, house. I was sobbing uncontrollably; couldn't regain my composure.

"What happened?" she asked, when I screeched in front of her house, barely missing a row of garbage cans.

'I don't know; I'm just so sad," I bawled.

Clara, who thankfully, is a psychologist, took the wheel and drove me straight to my doctor's office.

"You're having an episode," Dr. Easley whispered while stroking my back.

"What? I pulled my blouse tight against my chest, shielding myself against the dreadful words.

"Well, it's what some people call a 'nervous breakdown.' Take these pills. I'm going to write a prescription of anti-depressants for you."

For several months, Clara doubled as friend and personal psychologist. She would pick me up to accompany her on errands, appointments and shopping.

In my lowest moments, when depression made me want to isolate, God so lovingly sent me Clara who refused to let me fade away. She was my antidote.

I think back to how Clara and I met. We were in a business meeting, both pursuing licenses in Finances. She was a bit impersonal, while her husband was the socializer.

I looked forward to seeing her husband, Gerald, who was always comical and good-natured. So, it was Gerald who God used to bring Gerald and I together.

Years later, Gerald unexpectedly passed away. Clara was his only family member living in New York; the others resided in Philadelphia. Not wanting Clara to grieve alone, I moved in with her for almost a month, to lend a hand to my beloved friend.

God often sends help through people, prayer or circumstances, reminding us that we're never truly alone.

I was there for Clara in her need. Now Clara is sent to help me through my dark moments.

Lord, I ask that You continue to send Your angels to guard me from danger, shield me from harm, and guard my daily steps.

CHAPTER TEN

Faith Is Powerful

"Now faith is the substance of things hoped for, the evidence of things not seen."
Hebrews 11:19 (KJV)

It was once a nice place to live, but recent events have changed this seven-building development where I, my sons and my boyfriend reside. When I moved there, it housed a laundromat, mini-supermarket and even a shoemaker – all the amenities of an upscale development.

The landlord tried to keep the buildings in an unspoiled condition. Unfortunately, some tenants' children kept breaking the buzzers on the entrance door; busting out lights on the staircases; peeing in the elevators; and most egregiously, selling drugs in the buildings.

It was definitely time to go! My sons are young – just 7 and 14 years old. Their minds were easily influenced by their environment, and these surroundings were a horrible influence.

And so, I started searching for a new place to live and hated every step of the process.

My realtor would call me with a possible rental. I would hurry home from work to meet him, get the 'It's been taken' response from the landlord and repeat the process again.

I began to feel there was some "favoritism" from landlords at play, and it surely wasn't in my favor. I decided to ask my Italian friend, Carly, to join in the search with me.

Meanwhile, I started packing. I would carry boxes home from work on the train daily. My curious neighbors would ask where I was moving. When I told them that I didn't know, they thought I was keeping it private. Understandable. Who would pack to move without knowing where they are going? Me!

I felt a sense of urgency to move out. I didn't see it yet, but a storm was on its way. And God had been preparing me for it.

One day, I'm approaching the building after work. The neighbors are outside, loud and frenzied.

"What's going on? Another drug bust?" I asked balancing moving boxes and groceries in my arms.

"No, you didn't hear? Kyle's little sister, Vicky, came home from school and Kyle was on the couch. He was dead from a gunshot to the head."

Kyle was my 14-year-old's friend. A great kid he hung out with daily. I was even friendly with his mother. Kyle is dead!

From that day on, Carly and I ramped up my apartment search with a vengeance.

One day Carly called me at work. "I got something that sounds good. Meet me after work," she said. Her voice was an octave higher than usual.

I met Carly carrying a stock-pile of boxes from work.

"My sister knows this lawyer who has a house and is looking for a tenant," she said.

Carly and I then put a strategy in place.

"This is what we do. Carly, you act like you're the one who's looking for the apartment, and see if the landlord says it's taken. Then we'll know if he's discriminating or not," I said.

We arrive on a tree-lined street in Park Slope, Brooklyn. Mr. Vanderbilt, a tall, slender, silver-haired white man steps outside of the Brownstone house.

"Is the apartment still available?" Carly blurted.

"Yes, it's still available," Mr. Vanderbilt said.

That was my cue to reveal that it was me who was inquiring about the apartment.

"I live in a development but am looking for a more private environment. Too many people," I chuckle.

I omitted the occurrence of a death, vandalism, drug-dealing and shoot-out, including a police helicopter on the roof of my building. Mr. Vanderbilt might conclude that I was desperate.

Truth is, I was.

"I'm taking applications. Where do you work?" he asked.

"I work for a law firm, Williams Ellison."

"Oh, I have cases with them. Sit down," he said, pointing us in the direction of two wicker chairs.

"So, who do you work for at the firm"? Mr. Vanderbilt inquired.

"Thomas Manco."

"Really? I currently have a case with him. We're the defendants in the Marks v. Taylor case. We have a court date on Wednesday."

"Wow, this is such a coincidence. I've been working for Thomas for ten years."

"Well, if you want the apartment, it's yours," Mr. Vanderbilt stated with finality.

"It's two bedrooms. The rent is $750 a month and you can move in on the 1st." He walked us to the door and shook my hand.

No application was ever filled out.

Two weeks later, I'm sitting at my desk at work and someone taps me on the shoulder.

"Oh, hi Mr. Vanderbilt," I said.

Who needs an application when your prospective landlord could just come to your job and verify your employment.

We did move in on the 1st of the month, and lived in that brownstone in a beautiful area of Brooklyn, for three years.

~~

Packing those boxes was evidence of my faith in God during trials and hardships. I was fighting for my sons' lives and future. No way was I going to allow them to become a statistic of this threatening environment.

Every storm that loomed in my life carried both fear and promise. I was learning to trust the One who calms my fears and delivers His promises.

CHAPTER ELEVEN

Lean on Him

"Trust in the Lord with all thine heart, and lean not unto thine own understanding:
Proverbs 3:5-6 (KJV)

As my rent climbed, so did my confidence to achieve homeownership.

I believed that if I could pay the $1,000 rent, I could also handle a mortgage. Of course, I needed a home with rental space to help with the monthly payments. But I believed it was doable.

So, I start looking for a house with a rentable apartment.

Toby, my realtor called me during my work day with some leads. I rushed to meet him after work, some days leaving early.

Unfortunately, he took me to see some houses that I know he wouldn't even buy. After the fourth one, I had really had it.

I was so 'hot' when he called me the next day.

"Do not take me to any houses you wouldn't buy yourself. The last house was tearing away from the foundation and should have been condemned. I make more damn money than you do. What makes you think I want some condemned-looking houses in the ghetto?"

How dare him!

In the meantime, I'm sharing my dream of homeownership with family and friends.

Nobody meant any harm. I know they were trying to protect me. Unfortunately, they were projecting their limitations, fears or lack of vision onto me, but I was steadfast in my decision to be a homeowner. I intended to show my sons the benefits of working hard to achieve their goals.

"What you gonna do if the boiler breaks?"

"You don't have anybody to fix things if they break."

"What if your tenant doesn't pay rent?"

"You don't know who people are when they move in. You know they lie."

"Butchie and his family need a place to stay. You should let them stay with you."

"Those people don't want you in their neighborhood."

Their negativity echoed around me and felt never-ending, but God's promises became my anchor.

One day, Toby called me at work. It was 12:30 and I was leaving for lunch.

"Please don't hang up. I have a four-family building in foreclosure for you to look at. My friend in the bank told me to come over asap. Please, please just look at it. I won't steer you wrong. Meet me at 3:00 pm today and bring a check with you."

I looked in my wallet for the ever-present check I carried, just in case. I then called my friend, Henry, to come with me.

~~

"The owner is old and doesn't have the income to pay the mortgage. His daughter and her boyfriend have 'dogged' the place out. I think they're druggies," Toby said, pushing open the entrance door.

Inside the house looked as if it had been vacant for years. There were no lights on, no heat, old worn-out furniture in the four musty-smelling apartments and moldy, shabby, frayed carpet in the common areas.

"Are you serious?"

Before I could really verbally 'let loose' on Toby, Henry pulled me by the arm.

"Excuse us for a sec," he said.

"Listen. You are focusing on cosmetic stuff. These things can be fixed with plaster and paint. Do you know what's happening in this area?"

"And do you see that condemned factory across the street? It probably has dope fiends and crackheads living in there," I protested.

"Well, do you know what's going to happen to that condemned factory? They're going to build condos or something else there, and the value of all of these houses are going to skyrocket," Henry pleaded.

"I don't know. This place will take a lot of work before I can rent it out."

"Girl, if you don't write him a check to hold it for you, he will find somebody else before you get home. I might even try to get it myself. Are you kidding me?"

I reached in my bag and wrote the bank a check for $10,000, scared out of my mind. Thankfully, I took advantage of the savings plans on my jobs. It was for such a time as this.

I was walking in fear instead of faith, not yet knowing the fullness of God's power.

~~

A month later, I'm in a meeting when I meet Justin. He was learning the finance business part-time.

"What do you do full time?" I ask.

"Oh, I do construction. I work with a company that renovates houses."

"Do you work on any jobs on the side?"

"Of course. Gotta have a side hustle," said the young, muscular Justin.

For the next twenty years, Justin and his team have rebuilt and maintained my home. Their expertise has transformed a 'hot mess' of a dilapidated house to a stylish, warm, inviting, home.

I am thankful that I didn't let others' fears hold me back. My dreams were bigger than their doubts.

God always strengthens us and sends support when you need it most.

CHAPTER TWELVE

Girls' Trip

"He that speaketh in an unknown tongue edifieth himself"
1 Corinthians 14:4 (KJV)

One summer during a 'Shop Til You Drop' trip, I received a gift far greater than any sale, bargain or discount imaginable.

My friend, Grace, and I were walking through the narrow hallway of the 'package deal' hotel.

"Let's drop the bags in the room and get something to eat," Grace said.

"Okay, but don't you dare sit down. You know you'll fall asleep like a baby."

As we navigate through the winding narrow path of the hallway, we stopped suddenly.

"You hear that?" she whispered.

"Yeah, it sounds like the chanting in the movie "Rosemary's Baby." But I know they're speaking in tongues. It's a gift from God. I heard it in a Baptist church before."

We inched closer to the room and peered through a slight opening in the door.

Formed in a circle, was a group of people chanting and praying in Spanish.

I grabbed Grace's arm, "Come on, let's get out of here."

Hearing us, a man dressed in a long, black robe, pulled the door open wider.

"Please join us. All are welcome," he said, smiling broadly.

"No, we're okay. We were just passing by when we heard you," I said. I tugged at Grace's arm, more aggressively this time.

"Alright, just for a little while," Grace said.

I shot her a 'you traitor' look and walked towards the circle.

I was then escorted to the middle of the circle. The leader placed his hand on my forehead.

Then, in a low, soothing, melodic voice, he said:

"Repeat these words–
There is no one better than you.
There is no one better than you.
Please open your mouth.
There is no one better than you.
Let the words flow.
Open up wide."

I obliged and opened my mouth, breathing slowly through my mouth to calm my nerves.

Astonished, I heard a loud chant. It sounded as if it was coming from me, but my lips weren't moving. It was like the "Rosemary's Baby" chanting.

My next memory was of the group standing above me in prayer, as I lay on the carpeted hotel room floor.

I squinted to focus, and saw Grace standing above me behind one of the women.

A young man gently lifted me by the arm, pulling me to my feet.

"How do you feel?" he asked.

"Strange," I replied.

"I know. It's a beautiful experience. What a blessing," he said, leading me by the arm to the door.

"Please come again. We'll be here all weekend spreading God's Word. God bless you."

"Girl," Grace said, as we grabbed our bags near the door and left the room.

"What? That was some strange stuff," I said.

"Girl, you were speaking in tongues. What the heck? Then your ass fell head first and passed out."

"I don't know. This whole thing is so weird. It was like an outer body experience," I shook my head.

"You know what? I'm gonna call your ass 'Saint Sylvia' from now on," Grace teased.

"You better not. Just pray to me from now on," I laughed.

I was unsteady on my feet, dazed and overall shocked to the core. We walked arm-in-arm towards the eateries.

"No words, I have no words," I said.

"I'm not saying it's a bad thing. Just a weird thing. Let's eat before I get too hangry," Grace said.

That nudge was God's way of getting my attention. He steered me in the path of that room to show that He had something very special for me.

I have since learned to listen for the nudges that guide, warn or encourage me.

I thank God for trusting me with the gift of speaking in tongues. It's a powerful reminder that the Holy Spirit lives and moves within me.

This gift wasn't wrapped and tied with a bow, but it was priceless!

CHAPTER THIRTEEN

The Turning Point

"And be not conformed to this World: but be ye transformed by the renewing of your mind..."
Romans 12:2 (KJV)

I walked back to the doctor's office with a foreboding sense of dread. The memory of that day is forever etched in my mind.

I had just left the office for my follow-up appointment after surgery. The insurance company finally conceded that the breast reduction was essential for medical reasons.

I was healing well, so I was clueless why the doctor was summoning me back to his office.

"I owe you some money?" I joked, masking my agitation.

"Please have a seat," Dr. Fine directed.

He sat down in a chair opposite me, with a discomfiting stare for a second or two.

"I just received a call from the pathologist who examined the tissue we removed from you. They found cancer in your right breast."

Then in cinematic slow motion, Dr. Fine moved to impose an awkward, lingering hug on me.

I think I wiggled myself free of his embrace. I then walked back to my car in a haze, and wept without constraint on my son's shoulder.

I never imagined that I would become a cancer patient. I consistently had mammograms, and diligently practiced self-care.

Upon reflection, my sense of urgency to get the surgery was a nudge from the Holy Spirit. He wanted to reveal the cancer hiding in my breast.

I've learned that understanding why things happen isn't necessary to have faith. All I need to know is that God will carry me through it.

And knowing that, I can't help but share how good He's been to me.

~~

The medical transport van retrieved me five days a week, for months, to receive radiation treatments.

The breast cancer was revealed in a beginning stage. A series of radiation treatments and medication were proposed to eliminate and prevent any further spread of the cancer.

I kept my diagnosis a secret, only telling my closest family members and friends. I thought maybe I'll tell others later. I don't want the questions, comments or sympathy.

But God had other plans.

> *"Many are the plans in a person's heart, but it is the Lord's purpose that prevails."*
> **Proverbs 19:21**

CHAPTER FOURTEEN

The Awakening

*"Carry each other's burdens, and in this way,
you will fulfill the law of Christ"*
Galatians 6:2 (KJV)

In treatment facilities, there is a tradition of "ringing the bell" by the cancer patients. It symbolizes the final treatment session for their cancer.

"I'm going to ring the crap out of that bell tomorrow," I told Carl, the technician.

On the final morning, I'm sitting on my bed, easing into the subtle aches of climbing out of bed.

I had already decided only to tell close family and friends about my diagnosis. It was nobody's business. That was my plan!

As I put my feet on the floor, I hear:

"Share your story. It will help others," the Holy Spirit whispered.

On May 21, 2025, I rang the bell declaring my final radiation treatment. I sang "Ring My Bell" while I did a 'happy dance' to celebrate the occasion.

Returning home, I was excited about being obedient to the Holy Spirit. I posted a picture of me ringing the bell and captioning my thanks to God. I didn't do it for 'likes,' heart emojis, or happy faces on social media.

I shared my story to show the goodness of God.

Going back to my business meetings, I found myself encircled by some female associates. We gathered in a corner and I shared how the cancer was revealed to me. I explained how the cancer had been hiding, but was revealed by the Holy Spirit.

Like me, some were told that the spot on their mammogram x-ray was an indication of their dense breasts. I encouraged them to follow up and get second opinions.

In my hardest season, God placed people in my path who carried me when I couldn't carry myself. Now, God is using me to reach out, comfort and lift others as I was once lifted.

He turned my trials into a ministry of compassion.

Upon reflection, I realize God has softened my heart and

opened my eyes to the frailties of humanity. Though my journey wasn't easy, I love my parents and the adults who invested in my life. And with time, I've learned to see their flaws through grace. I realize they were doing the best they could with the human limitations they possessed, not a lack of love.

And through God's grace, I'm becoming the adult, the parent, and the child of God that He always intended.

Instead of judging, I choose to understand, to see others through His eyes of grace and compassion.

Each day, I see life with faith and gratitude, trusting that His goodness will always shine through.

CHAPTER FIFTEEN

Thank You

"Give thanks in all circumstances; for this is God's will for you in Christ Jesus."
1 Thessalonians 5:18 (KJV)

Months later, I'm on the bus on an 80-degree October day. Yes, it's unusual to be 80 degrees in October, but I accept change as a way of life now.

I knew it would be a challenge getting to church. The bus only runs hourly on Sundays. So, I wore sneakers and bought a cup of coffee to sip while waiting.

Whatever it takes, I have to go and say "Thank You" in the Lord's house, and fellowship with His believers.

When I arrive at my church, known as "the church with the long lines" in Canarsie, Brooklyn, I was pleasantly surprised to discover that it's Communion Sunday. I'm excited to worship the body and blood of Jesus.

My cries that Sunday are of joy, love and surrender. I'm feeling gratitude for the Lord who never abandoned me. His steadfast love keeps me anchored.

~~

As I close this chapter of my life, I know His presence strengthens and comforts me through my fears and challenges.

He has carried me through trials and storms that I thought could never be endured. I stand not because of my strength, but because of the Lord's faithfulness.

My story was never in the world's hands. God is the Author of my life, and He's already written the next chapter with purpose and grace.

God's love is enough to sustain me while I wait.

Thank you, thank you, My Heavenly Father.

Prayer:

"I thank You, Father, for never leaving me, for nurturing my spirit, and for the promise that as I seek You, I will find You.

Grow me, Lord, in faith, in hope, and in Your everlasting love. In Jesus' name, I pray. **Amen**.*"*

BOOKS BY SYLVIA DIANE MITCHELL

PINK FRIDAY: (PART 1 OF SERIES TRILOGY)
LAVENDER: (PART 2 OF SERIES TRILOGY)
SILVER SALVATION: (PART 3 OF SERIES TRILOGY)

AND HER LATEST BOOK

**GOD IS WRITING MY STORY, NOT THE WORLD –
GRACE IN EVERY TRIAL**

(A SPIRITUAL MEMOIR)

FIND ALL PUBLICATIONS AT

AMAZON AND BARNES & NOBLE

NOTES

NOTES

NOTES

NOTES

NOTES

NOTES

NOTES

NOTES

NOTES

NOTES

NOTES

NOTES

NOTES

www.ingramcontent.com/pod-product-compliance
Lightning Source LLC
Chambersburg PA
CBHW050656160426
43194CB00010B/1965